UNDERSTATEMENT

UNDERSTATEMENT

An Anthology of Twelve Poets

Edited by Tanya Nanavati

Seraphim Editions

Copyright © The Authors

Published in 1996 by
Seraphim Editions
1000 Gerrard Street East
P.O. Box 98174
Toronto, Ontario
M4M 3L9

Canadian Cataloguing in Publication Data

ISBN 0-9699639-3-9

1. Canadian poetry (English)—20th century.
I. Nanavati, Tanya.

PS8279.U53 1996   C811'.5408   C96-900737-X
PR9195.25.U53 1996

PRINTED AND BOUND IN CANADA

Page Layout by Norman Skinner

Special thanks to Susan Becker

Table of Contents

Nacia Miller

Nedra

Acknowledgments

Introduction

Poetry is immediate in its route to the senses. It is deeply rooted in childhood experiences, when we are more directly in touch with the language of dreams and the unconscious. As Wordsworth observes in his *Intimations of Immortality*, the child comes "trailing clouds of glory," but the "glory" fades, and "shades of the prison-house begin to close" as that child grows into adulthood.

In our society today, that childhood world of the tactile and the unconscious seems unbearably fragile. Wordsworth's "glory" seems to trail off into a "prisonhouse" of severely limited attention spans, passive entertainment, virtual reality and interaction through electronics. Language and its rich textures and layers are lost in the flash and glitz of a high-tech, one-dimensional world. As an antidote to this, against all odds, the art of poetry continues to flourish.

Poetry is the path back to ourselves. Therefore, it should be accessible and immediate, not cloaked in an intellectualism that renders it obscure and removed from the senses of the reader. Poetry should be heard and experienced; not read in analytical terms in a static, scholarly environment, but spoken, and lived and breathed. It is the art that speaks to everyone. There are no guidelines to follow to immerse oneself in the sensual pleasure of living in a poem. The spirit of discovery in poetry is the discovery of oneself.

Our responses to poetry are subjective: though a good poem goes beyond an individual response and holds universal appeal; and a great poem has the power to touch all who come into contact with it. Reading is an active experience; reading poetry goes beyond that. It becomes a connected flowing of memories, emotions and experiences between the poet and the reader. Poetry lives in the tactile images of the senses; it lives through sound, metaphor, rhythm and cadence; and we relate to it through our own emotional centre.

When I hear a poet read his or her work, I connect with the message I hear, and the response that rises up in me to meet it. The union of poet and listener/reader is as unique as a fingerprint; an active, internal experience, in which language is the medium. To paraphrase Ronna Bloom, the job of a poem is to have a different life in the heart and mind of every reader. Each word contains its literal meaning, as well as a storehouse of associated meanings; the memories it links you to, the magic of its sound, the traditional or archetypal associations it triggers, its personal emotional trail, its allusions and shadows.

I love the world that opens up with one word or phrase, like Blake's choir of angels, when one reaches that mystical, unseen place revealed by the rhythm and the resonances of the language. I love when the words in the poem I'm reading embody a feeling that seems to have flown directly from inside me. I love the link between my below-the-surface world, and that of the poet.

What is left unsaid in a poem is almost as important as what is stated. Like the negative space in a painting, the 'understatements' illuminate the image we see, and give it the added depth and clarity that echo in our own unconscious. The underlife of a poem is doubly rich; in the subliminal world of the poet as well as that of the reader.

In this anthology of twelve poets, their diversity of background and experience leave dramatic and distinct imprints on the underside of their work. The rich variety of style and subject reflect the diversity of the the Toronto area, where poetry through the so-called venue of the Spoken Word is undergoing a resurgence. They write of love and hate, death, divorce, feminism, racism, fanaticism, terrorism, injury and recovery, joy and despair, childbirth, children, parents, lovers, sensuality, technology, alienation, self-discovery, memory... Their poetry is immediate, dynamic and diverse; their art flourishing in a mean-spirited political environment that decries the arts as extraneous, rather than as nourishment for the spirit.

We may aspire to be poets in our hearts, but very few of us are inspired enough to articulate these thoughts into language. As Tennyson laments in *Break, Break, Break*, "I would that my tongue could utter the thoughts that arise in me." The utterances in this collection touch, awaken and enlighten; they exemplify the idea of the poet being the heartbeat of society, and of the timelessness of the art form, where in Shelley's words, the "singing still dost soar, and the soaring ever singest."

Tanya Nanavati

Ronna Bloom

Ronna Bloom is a Toronto poet and psychotherapist. Her poetry has appeared in numerous Canadian journals including *Queen's Quarterly*, *WRIT*, *The Canadian Forum* and *Grain*. Her first collection, *Fear of the Ride*, will be published in the fall of 1996 by Harbinger Poetry Series at Carleton University Press.

This Poem Contains Nudity

Write me, it whispers,
inviting. Write me now.

Oh, I couldn't, I say. I am shy.
I hardly know you.
Your conventions, your breath.
It is too intimate.

Tiptoe through me in ankle bracelets.
Pluck my lines from vines like grapes
and hold me in your mouth.
I want you to know me
from the inside.

I am scared.

In its unwritten state, the poem
is naked, stripped of clothes, of body.
It has no shame, exists without form,
wants a body to enter the world with, any body.

The poem isn't coy, it is wide open.
I am the prude with the pen, the one
trying to fit its huge expanse of self through this
small inky orifice.

Write me, it whispers.
Write me now.

Ronna Bloom

Landlady

My landlady was coming up from the basement,
from the dark cement underground
where I've never been, where
all the incinerator shafts connect and collect the garbage.
She was coming up those steps, fat
probably two hundred and fifty pounds of her, full of all
of her self, filled right out to the edge
of her skin, her long brown hair straight
down, past her waist, past
her back, draped over her shoulders, straight
and swirling at the same time she was
coming up the stairs on a shell, floating
into the daylight out of the basement
on her slow feet I couldn't see them
for the concrete wall between us, she
was floating out of there like the Birth
of Venus. God she was beautiful.

The Weaving

You are a new thread of colour
wispy like hair, spiral
featherlike around my body, barely
touching the back of my neck
behind my ears, whispering
yourself into my pattern.

This colour—I don't know
its name. It is fire white
after image purple. It is a handful
of clay, so blue.

My pattern has its pattern:
knots and waves, ancient
spirals. The path is not clear,
the pattern still in motion, weaving itself and you
are a part of it.

I imagine when I am dead, someone
will find the weaving among my books
notice this strand of you and ask:
What is this colour called
and why is there so little, why this
intense flash and then no more?

Or else, gathering, marvel
at the sudden change in texture, tone, saying:
See how it explodes here in the middle
after the greys and blacks, the rich wines and blues,
one fine thread of fire was woven in
and the whole piece is brilliant.

Ronna Bloom

Blue Raft[*]

My sister's bed a blue raft
dim in street light. Cars drive past
carrying their own whispered news.
I've put the kids to sleep.
Snow moves over this family
of households. The Pluto nitelite
comforting the hall.
In my sleep, I hear the ring
of numberless telephones, hear
the hospital and the clocked breathing
of my niece. Tonight
I am the guardian of the ordinary. I wake
before the phone does, knowing her dead.

---

[*] From the series "What A Kick Feels Like"

This Clean*

I go to a party, the last day sitting shiva. Everyone a stranger. I look at men. Nobody tall. It doesn't matter. I want a body, hide in the kitchen from the idea. The word inappropriate comes in on a platter with toothpicks and I go into the hall. There are men there too. Everywhere there's combed-in musk and wrist bone. Apples moving in throats. In the basement there are fingers netting the air. I want to be that air. Want someone to know I've been in mourning, want no one to know I've been touched. I'm clean. No one will be this clean again. Death takes everything out of you. Put it back, put it back. Everywhere there's fragrance, everywhere judgement. Who do you tell you've just buried a five year old and sex is on your mind.

---

* From the series "What A Kick Feels Like"

Soft Skin

They went to bed and spent there fifty years
watching their skin loosen and thin. So that
whole patches of leg could be rubbed without ever
moving the muscle. Lying thinnish skin on thin skinnish
and rub. Moving yet, moving still
the tongues. Talk and talk and lick soft skin
loose talk easy licking. Still steamy.

Things Seen in Kensington Market

The kidney beans and pinto beans, the colour
of adzuki beans, their purplishness
in the five o'clock light. So many types of rice
and the prices, fifty nine cents a pound. The breads
down the road. One single pumpernickel that had burst
its form, insides exploding the skin of crust, calling out:
Buy me. Buy me.
A small consideration of cinnamon buns.
A taste of fruitcake.
The walk down Augusta.
I hadn't been there in the darkening
in the dark, I hadn't been there at night before.
It looked different with the ability to see clearly
inside stores, my eyes drawn to the bloody
animals stripped and hung in the butcher window,
a plate of pig noses, a box of feet, another one
of crowded livers, the sound
electric saw, continuous and high-pitched, police
cars outside. I tried on a skirt
in a second-hand store,
red crinkly fabric that slung off me,
would swirl if I danced.

The Job of An Apple

The job of an apple is to be hard,
to be soft, to be crisp, to be red,
yellow and green. The job of an apple is to be pie,
to be given to the teacher, to be rotten.
The job of an apple is to be bad
and good, to be peeled, cored, cut,
bitten and bruised. The job
of an apple is to pose for painters,
roll behind fridges, behind grocery aisles,
to be hidden, wrapped in paper,
stored for months, brought out in the dry heat
of India and eaten like a treasure.
The job of an apple is to be
handed over in orchards, to be wanted
and forbidden. The job of an apple is to be Golden
Delicious, Granny Smith and crab. The job
of an apple is to be imported, banned and confiscated
going through customs from Montreal to New York.
The job of an apple is to be round. Grow. Drop.
To go black in the middle when cut. To be thrown
at politicians. To be carried around for days. To change
hands, to change hands, to change hands.
The job of an apple is to be a different poem in the mouth
of every eater. The job of an apple is to be juice.

Robert Boates

Robert Boates is the author of *The Afterlife* a documentation of a man's first five years of recovery from a severe brain injury. He provides a literary voice for survivors and their families and friends, recording the endless, arduous road towards recovery.

Robert shared the top prize in a National Poetry Competition sponsored by Fame Canada Enterprises of Victoria, B.C., with his entry "Late September." His first collection of poetry, *The Good Life* (a work in progress), was published by Cactus Tree Press, 1990.

A native of Hamilton now living in Toronto, Robert learned long ago that once a poem is written, the reasons behind it cease to matter, for the poem then acquires a life of its own.

Man Without Memory

Watching poplars sweep the sky
dahlias withering in a garden,
two flamingos in tableau.
I know nothing of this place
or of seasons.

When you enter the room
I forget the world outside.
I check my watch;
I have been awake two minutes
and must write it down.
You are the first person
I have ever seen,
ever held, ever spoken to.

You produce a diary and a pen.
In the book are entries
by my hand, but I did not
write them; I have never seen
this book before, never written
a single word
anywhere.

You press me on the penmanship
which we both recognize,
and I reiterate, to distraction,
that I have never seen the book before.
I have never seen you before this moment.
I know nothing of nurses or illness.

I check my watch:
I have been awake two minutes.
I don't remember your arrival.
Before me is a deck of cards
laid out on a bed.
Someone is playing Patience.

Again you ask about the journal,
lined with scores of music.
This enrages me
for I have never written or conducted
though you assure me once I sang.
I know nothing of song or supplication.

I check my watch against yours:
I have been awake
for only two minutes;
I have just been born:
Hello, Hello, I love you.

Declaration

This is a song of hate
I am growing stronger
Rapidly in wrath
Yellow alert
Prepare for war
You will not know
I am coming
I'm learning again to keep
pain to myself
A tortured innocent
No one heard it
from me
You were safe
But you destroyed my love
Your distance is no relief
I'm shackled to your genes
I tried running from blood
The nightmare began
decades ago
I know something about
the world of dreams
The other side of life
There was no ascension
in my rebirth
Speared for years
I am a hound of hell
galloping delightfully home

Prayer

How do I beg
for a silent pardon
Surely frustration
and despair were expected
My heart is wrapped
in broken glass but
I've made it this far
Am I to be laced
with horror all my life
Slower than a sloth
I cannot be a threat
Once I looked forward
to grandfatherhood
Do you require
a deeper story
I plead guilty
I've earned my shame
I owe my demoralized ally
She gave birth
to what I'm becoming
Raised me properly
in a second childhood
I cry out
in a robe she purchased
for this pilgrimage
Teach me how to fly
My eyes are wide open
and I am still flapping

Survivor

A priest says I'm brave,
but I wasn't strong
enough to let go.
It took this injury
to divide us.
That's how much
I love you.

A mute singer,
I remain
a man of words.

Forgive me
for not dying
completely.

The Afterlife

It's the aftermath
of child abuse
A severe head-injury
Love's destruction
It's losing a spiritual mate
Sobbing tear-ducts dry
Remorse and hatred
Living dead
It's abandonment
Sleeping in a bed
once shared
It's reoccurring dreams
of a grass widow wife
Counting the months
not knowing days of the week
Watching seasons come and go
Never seeing the children
It's a crazy Keeshond
who had to be put down
It's a dormant telephone
and Mormons at the door
It's life on welfare
and disability pension
Smoking tobacco again
It's tegratal for seizures
and prozac for depression
Waiting on the law
Returning to prayer
Keeping promises to God
and Geraldine

It's no longer asking
about reunion
It's not maybe someday
It's letting her go
alone in a journey
toward sanity

Resolution

I wasn't going to Heaven,
and saw no light
through a tunnel
in my coma.

Goblins of incest
watched us gleefully
while we attempted
to over-ride them.

You and I were defeated
by my drunken tumble
down illegal stairs
the day Dr. Singh
induced my recall
with his truth-serum.

The stairs were replaced
to avoid the law.
Needing to disappear,
I came this direction
for assimilation.

Forty

I now attend
T'ai Chi Ch'uan classes
The spine, lungs, and thighs
need the work

I practise rising
above the ashes
of life
with Geraldine

It was a long climb
out of a dry well
carrying *battered wings*
that *still kick up dust*

This is the end
of my beginning
The beginning
of another end

Continuum

Stopped waiting to hear
from my second wife
She will always see me
brain-injured
I am too disabled
for love
Was before the concrete
hit my head
I could make babies but
have never dealt well
with intimacy
Darwin said adapt or die
I've learned to walk lightly
and hope for the best

Allan Briesmaster

Allan Briesmaster has lived in Toronto since 1969. He was host and organizer of the weekly Art Bar Poetry Series in 1994-95, and continues his involvement in the series as well as actively supporting other Spoken Word events around the city. He led Phoenix Poets' Workshop in 1986-90. In the past few years he has been a featured reader at numerous venues across Southern Ontario. Eleven of his poems appear in the 6-poet anthology *Mix Six* (Mekler & Deahl, 1996). He is National Co-ordinator of the Canadian Poetry Association, and is one of the founders of *Scenes* magazine.

Tech vs. Earth

Imagine a white hand gripped
around the stony sphere our world:
the rotund arc of which
buckles, the grip's
that big and hard.
                    Blood
or a red sap drips from it,
from both, splashes off lost into space.
—From both. For the wounding hand too, partly
ruptures and is scarred, parts
get ripped
obstinately by the living and dead surface pieces,
by the breakage, the protrusions. (Hear
the leaky hiss? that bass
grumble-and-groan, high whine?)
But eaten also, through earth's own
more steady appetite, mouth
of the moth, deep joint-fatigue, a stealthy
freckling of rust...

Yet the mechanic hand just
regenerates, and flexes in, stiffens:
growing perpetually as though, had
it a brain
controlling it, that brain long
forgot how their wrist, for all
its girth, still roots
live nerve, veins, in the shrunken
violated tomb of earth.

Allan Briesmaster

The Luminous Man

I have this other self who stays
in hiding, quiet
under the fabric of my skin almost
not breathing.
When he slips out, he sheds
me like a mis-fit uniform:
to stride
the broad, the near, surrounding
shores of the bloodwarm gulf.

His acts
embody, gently,
old qualities I had thought lost.
—A fervor
unashamed in its own sinew.
Placid strength. A surety.
Intensest ease.

All because you, his consort,
answer,
and you call,
in kind. Lantern
of this flesh. Beckoner
to fallow fields of touch.
To simplest orchard, branching tree
where retuned pulses tremor
along the trunk's ascension
from the caress
by leafy fingertip. Secreted
flame. Liquid
enclosure. Smooth vined arms
and an irriguous
rich-earthen grip.

Toward aching sweet
convulsion of release.

And thereafter, the sea
has withdrawn into heights beyond
horizon, poured and steamed away,
to imbue sky, but also
sunken, far
inside the cavernous and grotto-like
primeval garden,
back to the limpid spring
cleft through the mantle-rock
with pooled flow deep and sure as any
canopy of marine air.

... Before
such fluid dissipates like sunset,
and selves of light remove
into auroral curtainfolds,
and reliquary lives
find we're congealed
among our surfaces once
more

Onion Brunch

Diced onion frying with that sharp
crackle, hiss and sizz
through butter light of Sunday noon
re-strings the mind

while watering the sides
of the tongue; and for
a moment, many such noons
tug and cinch, and we

are not in that apartment, and are not
those edgy selves, which
submerge in a slight flood
of comfort.

I do not see then, I
hear white cubes turn
transparent, limp and sweet
with lessened sound. Until

loud bubbly pouring-on of froth
of whisked eggs
threads mind and
an eager palate

other ways. —With various
add-ins, a chopped green pepper's own
taut odor, shredded parmesan
and always our pinches

of spice; perhaps
marjoram, definitely ground pepper,
enough salt. All
of whose mutable

flavours will make
this week's unique,
in the end more fleeting,
omelette:

oil-shiny, folded whole, browngolden-
done,
from kitchen out onto the dining
table of the mobile sun.

Allan Briesmaster

Regret's Edge

Over my centre
gapes this
absent birth.

A line to
sky and breath
was let
part, slip, go
plummet. Once.
And so

through my chalk cliff
run tremors
of his embryo

beating its
cage, howling: all
mouth, o
for any
hatch of air

... up tons
of wreckage piled
like a sea-dust
on some

polar,
unfathomable
floor.

Martin's Light

Fallen between that float
of blaze and drain
in umber—evening of
wan wind, shrivelled
    clarity;
        the flecks
of a few hard yellows up
a poplar, say;
all comfort, like a mist's
fur, flensed away...

How low, then,
goes the sun. A shaven glare
of sorrow shows us, to the bone,
any harvest's over, last night's frost
has charred the rinds
across the inner gardens.

One more gust from
a curdled heaven, and the last
youth of the light, odd
glimmered ember, veers its
instant on wind and
stills down
to final dying in ground.
... Though awhile, the earth
becomes an earth of leaves.

        *

Martin,
I'm suddenly shy about these
cadences. And sounds, less
than blown leaves.

Your speech
knifed, it
could hurt like city truth, and yet
autumn always was—you said—your
season, difficult
romantic that you stayed.
                              Fitting,
October death. Today ... five years.
Where
reach you now, after the three
live autumns I held back,
care giver, my artist friend, archer
of fire through haze.

Where, but down this
morass of ash?

                    *

A week beyond the stilted funeral
I pulled onto a sideroad
toward a stand
of tattery trees. Walked east, scuffed
rustlingly among stripped limbs, till
at a clearing I felt
you. Firm strike,
then gentle flash.

Turned.
            A levelling sun
had slowed along
a broken winding. It remembered
summer. Little beams
of brightened smoke stretched far through panes
hot crome, scarlet, of those young maples

that bloom last, knee-height.
With the bloodglow
within sumac. Humble
cathedral. Buttresses to house, frailly,
your light: its
hearted flare.

Pain light, a voluntary suffering,
slashed
past numb incense of air
and soil.
A beam soon to be

a piercing wink-out, then
tough wisp gone
off the clammy
slant ahead.
    But held
that moment, self-held by
strength of your care,
cohering
in rubyglow that bore,
      that bears
a power to haunt my centre more
than back-leak of my own
lost dawns. Than
wintry sunset due. Although

at once I hear you
laughing, "Lighten up, man," as
I offer, toward
what lives—will live—
deeper than earth, apart
from only sunny air,
      the stubbed,
the burnt-out digits of these words.

Powassan Suite

from day's oven, past
mud of leech, air of blackfly—
plunge ... in   cool amber

under my back, rich lake; ...
high-up through lashes,—this
flown sunbow

june midnight. —pressed
on every screen: immense
whine, ... and the million stars

predawn, waiting to slap
out   the mosquito at
my ear—   far looncall

lull in the bugs,
air   muggy, still; gloom ... bellying toward
... a gust — boom! — downpour

lake, through night spruce—
burnt silver. torc of cloud   adorns
halfgolden moon

cloudblown dark; —deepcool wave-
crested woods   hisses. calms
with flashing fireflies

Afua Cooper

Afua Cooper is a Jamaican born poet of African descent living and practising the art of poetry in Toronto, Canada. To date she has published three books of poetry, the last of which, *Memories Have Tongue* was the first runner-up for the 1992 Casa de las Americas prize in the English language category.

Afua's poetry has a strong sense of history and place, and seeks to integrate the inner and outer worlds. Interwoven in her work is a strong feminist consciousness. Afua has recorded her poetry on the album *Womantalk*. After writing poetry for many years, Afua is now working on a collection of short stories entitled *Waiting For the Moon*, a children's story *Fatima's Nightgown*, and a novel *The Rowing*.

In addition to her creative works, Afua is also pursuing a doctorate in history at the University of Toronto. Utilising her background in history she has co-authored a book, *Essays in African-Canadian Women's History* published by the University of Toronto Press (1994).

Womanhood

We who were thrust out of dark caverns
into a maddening light
We who know no truth
         no honour
we who go through this madness called life
into the estate of adulthood
crossing no dividing line
experiencing no period of transition
having no celebration for our puberty
                    our blood
No rites of passage
no lovesong
only a shameful quietude
an impatient sadness
Now here we hang—suspended
between madness, agony and absolute truth
becoming women
suddenly thrust into a sphere we do not understand
becoming women

Bird of Paradise

At dawn my mother stands on the hill
behind our house
and invokes the sun to rise
then she goes to the outdoor kitchen
and prepares tortillas and cocotea for our breakfast

My mother sells fruits and flowers in the market
stuff she grows with her own hands
she does not solicit customers
they come to her of their own volition
and at the end of each day
her items are all sold out

Now at age 42 my mother decides to stop having children
but not because her blood has ceased
"I have peopled the world with the numerous men
and women that my body has birthed," she says
"Now it's time for me to birth other things"

At times my mother's back and feet grow tired
so I anoint them with coconut oil
her feet are a detailed map
her back is the starapple tree outside our front door

My mother has never travelled abroad
but she knows tales of everyland
she says the flowers in her gardens
especially the ginger lily, orchids,
and the bird of paradise, bring her such tidings

My mother is short in stature
all her children tower above her
some do not even want to recognise
or acknowledge her as they pass by in the marketplace
they are ashamed of this fruit and flower woman
this woman who fed them milk and tortillas
to make them so strong
sometimes they mock her
"She looks like something out of a Rivera mural," they jest
but my mother does not hear
her ears are beyond their words.

In the evening when she grows weary
my mother sings lullabies to the sun to entice it to sleep
so the dark can come and we all be rejuvenated
"It's in the darkness that we grow strong," she tells us

How wise she is
this woman with a life that no one can capture
how essential she is
this woman who makes gardens flower
and who feeds us milk and tortillas
I watch her as she descends the hill to the marketplace
her skirt at her knee
her black hair flecked with grey

Woman A Wail

Woman a wail
di eart is in labour
woman a wail
creation in danger
woman a wail
di eart is in labour
and what shall she bring forth from her travail?
Her mountains shall roar and spit fire
her bowels shall move and cause the eart to split
from one end to another
our minds too shall be rent asunder
this woman shall avenge herself

Who is she that looketh forth as the morning,
fair as the moon, clear as the sun,
but terrible as an army with banners*

She wail an bawl
as she destroy but
she create again and again
she wail an shriek
as she bring forth
a new way of thinking
a new way of living
a new understanding
a new way of looking
and a new new new creation

---

* Song of Solomon, chap. 6, verse 10.

ah seh woman a wail
(she begin her dance of terror)
di eart is in labour
woman a wail
(her dance of fear)
creation in danger
and what shall she bring forth from her travail?
From the mouth of the Ganges
from the throat of the Yangtze
from the heart of the Niger
from the belly of the Amazon
she dance
she dance down lightning and thunder
she dance down brimstone and fire
she is a mighty earthquake
she is a non-stop hurricane
she dance
          and
                    dance
and   dance
          and
            dance and dance
She dance her dance of terror
she dance her dance of fear
look she dancing 'pon her toenail
she is a mighty whirlwind
dancing the world's end

ah seh
woman a waillll
the eart is in labour
woman a wail
creation in danger
woman a wa–eh–eh–eh–eh–ail
the eart is in labour
and what shall she bring forth from her travail
what shall she bring forth from her travail?
A new way fi do tings
a new way fi see tings
a new way of looking
a new understanding
and
A new Creation
A new Creation
A new Creation

The Power of Racism

The power of racism
the power of racism
the power of racism
is such that Neville who is six foot two and weighs 210
could be threatened with assault by three white children

The power of racism
the power of racism
the power of racism
is such that a Yusef Hawkins was killed in Brooklyn
due to the colour of his skin

the power of racism
the power of racism
the power of racism is such
that the ROM* could mount an African exhibition
without consulting Black people

---

* Royal Ontario Museum

And I Remember

And I remember
standing
in the churchyard on Wesleyan hill
standing and looking down on the plains
that stretched before me
like a wide green carpet
the plains full with sugar cane and rice
the plains that lead to the sea

And I remember
walking
as a little girl to school
on the savannahs of Westmoreland
walking from our hillbound village
along steep hillsides
walking carefully so as not to trip and plunge
walking into the valley

And I remember
running
to school on the road that cuts into the green carpet
running past laughing waters
running past miles of sugar cane and paddies of rice
running to school that rose like a concrete castle
running with a golden Westmoreland breeze

And I remember
breathing
the smell of the earth plowed by rain and tractors
breathing the scent of freshly cut cane
breathing the scent of rice plants as they send
their roots into the soft mud

and I remember
thinking
this is mine   this is mine
this sweetness of mountains
valleys
rivers
and plains
is mine
mine
mine

At the Centre

Today doves flew from my head
and my hair grew
the longing is gone from my body
and I'm filled with peace, perfect peace

No longer shall I speak of electrocuted poets
or the ones who inhaled gas until
they danced in the dizziness of death
But of brown women
who turn the soil with their hands
making vegetable gardens and tending fruit trees

Today I went into my storehouse
selected the choicest oil and anointed my body
wrapped myself in the rarest cloth
of a deep wine red
stood at my front gate
and words poured from my mouth in flaming chants

Today the craftsman has come
to make a design for me
of a woman sitting in deep repose
with doves flying from her head
He has made all the pieces and they fit
well together
I shall hang it at my window for all the world to see

Nancy Dembowski

Nancy Dembowski is an expatriate single mother who moved to Toronto, from the US in 1991. Shortly after arriving in Canada, Nancy began writing and, since then, has performed her poetry at countless venues including the AGO, The Word on the Street and The Scream in High Park. Her poetry appears in *Carnival: A Scream in High Park Anthology*, (edited by Peter McPhee for Insomniac Press) and was also included in Jill Batson's *Word Up* project which included a CD (Virgin Records), a video (MuchMusic) and a print anthology (Key Porter). One of her poems was used in the play *Put Me Away*, (directed by Adam Nashman, written and performed by Lisa Ryder) which appeared at Buddies and Bad Times for the 1995 Fringe Festival. Her poetry has also appeared in *Kuntgeist*, *Oversion* and *SinOverTan* Magazines.

You'll Never Get Them Both in Bed:
Mom is Mom & Jesus is Dead

My back to a navy blanket. The plane comes down on me like: my
foot to the gas, Wild Turkey, you.

And last night, as I pranced deadpan from one tavern to the next
that same wind blew off those friends of yours
bits of frozen pea, corn, lima beans shooting out of their mouths.

I have more in common with people
who surround themselves with mechanical trash.

Corner a boy
sweating in the dank light
his dark eyes locked on top button of my blouse
his sheets drenched in everything about you
I'm glad to be rid of.

I paint the walls orange and dress like a pilgrim.

I'm not with the program.
I don't have a clue.
I'm over coddling and saving you.

Nancy Dembowski

Sweets

The waiter cracks an egg:
our salads sit
we take the stairs
our room is a museum
he's dressed his gift of chocolates in his Sunday shirt
I wear it open and alone
the skin of his eyes, his cheeks, sweet with aperitif
I drink quickly, and think
he is the lover of my life
this is the most elegant room I have ever been in
in my life.

My mother's house was simple:
butterscotch in coloured glass
no chandeliers to dress me in rainbows
only brother's prisms on the window sills
in some way equated with his love of symbols.

My husband calculates our travels:
I wait outside the door
I am mad for Japanese lanterns and American flags
summers, thieving ice creams and pencils
minus brother's brilliance in my hands
words were nothing next to numbers.

I keep my lover's chocolates in my bag
and find a place where I am close enough to watch
like a movie:
There is blood on the sidewalk
and bars on the window
I count, to the flicker of cars
while his hands undress my chocolates
and the money tumbles out.

Trash

Thought I saw your face on the back of a cereal box, and I
knew what to do with you;
emptied you out and filled you up with the bottle of aspirin
I bought
cause I don't own a car   and have an electric oven.
Then I flattened you with my butch boots
dumped you out in the dumpster behind the *Yes-I-Will*
bridal salon,
kitty-corner to the health food store
where I went to see the 90 year old psychic healer
who fondled me for 275 bucks of my own money.

Then again... I've been fine for 7 months now.
So I guess my money was well spent   and I'm not such a
fool after all.
Felt good   seeing you laying in all that lacy garbage.
I'll feed our children from trash cans if that's what it takes
being that our daughter carved dead bodies in the sand at
the McDonald's Playland.

Thought I found Jesus in a man   but then I got the idea
god must be a woman. Always was a rebel.
Forgot that somewhere between our vows and the booze
I've been leaning on lately.

He took me into Eliot and opera
and somehow his kisses   against my tears   and my eyes
staring into that stale box of Cheerios
helped me see your face carved in sand.

It Wasn't Until Later

Tried to die once for this. Makes me smile now to think of it, the overacted artlessness, the desperation of my spirit then, though I can't recall the pain I must have been in. How it felt to be in love with him. How it hurt to know I wasn't wanted. Enough to put a razor to my wrist, sit by the ocean door and wait for my life to end.

And a dying man, a young, sick, dying man, came to comfort me. Would have traded him my ace for his jack, even then I knew you were in store for what was left of me. The magazine girl in our bed had made it all come clean, with her cigarette and her fashion sense, she'd been certain what it was he really needed.

I knew then how cold I'd have to be and I just didn't want it. Couldn't tell you why it was I changed my mind: I was probably just afraid to die. And I laughed out loud at the fat nurse and her sadistic grin, judging me by a picture of him. And I knew I'd live. And I'm glad I did, tho he showed no pity for me, took no interest in my bandaged limbs. It wasn't until later he was sorry. After I'd been gone awhile. Suffering counted then, now it was his instead of mine. And now I'm through with you no doubt you'll change your tune, be as broken as he was then, as certain it was all your fault. And I'll be as faultless, heartless, bored with you, tho I wanted to explain: I didn't want this end. I'd wanted to be dead.

Autumn's Surrender

Pumpkins were gracing the fruit stands
when my grandmother died,
leaving only a handkerchief bunny as her immortal gift.
The previous summer she had sat stubbornly
beneath our overripe cherry tree
tho such a hive of bees had taken over;
even the beekeeper was taken aback.
Tonight, Cassiopeia winks at me,
her moon against the endless black-blue sky.
The cold is welcoming.
And it was autumn too when I surrendered,
my husband, laughing,
offering up some anecdotal amusement:
The intimacy stood awkwardly against our past.
Compassion came over me.
I wanted to borrow grandmother's courage
or Bonnie's,
her slow body unable to care for any of her five children:
"Here's my Maggie," she says,
"A little chubby in the cheeks like your Kelly."
The girl's dimpled face smiles up
from the cheap plastic photo album.
I do not know Bonnie well.
Her death will only graze me.
Her death will fall away
as brown leaves surrender to the winter night.

Carla Hartsfield

Carla Hartsfield was born in Waxahachie, Texas, a farming community south of Dallas. Before immigrating to Canada in 1982, she completed two performance degrees (Bachelor's and Master's) in piano at the University of Texas at Austin. Since that time she has established herself as a writer, performer and teacher. Carla Hartsfield has published in *Toronto Life, The Malahat Review, The Fiddlehead, Dandelion, Arc, Scrivener, The Carleton Arts Review, Index,* among others. In July 1996, her most recent book, *Fire Never Sleeps,* was added to the permanent collection at Smith College (Mortimer Rare Book Room—the largest holding of Plath papers in the world) due to her sequence of poems based on the journals and letters of Sylvia Plath. Carla Hartsfield has also just completed her first novel with the working title of *Crossing The Trinity,* set in Dallas. Currently, she teaches at the Royal Conservatory of Music in Toronto, and is still active as a piano soloist and chamber musician.

Publications:
The Invisible Moon (1988) Signal Editions/Vehicule
The Signal Anthology (1993) Signal Editions/Vehicule
Fire Never Sleeps (1995) Signal Editions/Vehicule

Dandelions

They are crowded and globular,
a Van Gogh painting.
I am level with their yellowness,
a color I hate.

Wildly bright
like a Warhol silkscreen,
they are also drugs,
aurora borealis.

They are fireworks slowly exploding,
and I wait for their burned-out stems
and colorless webs to imprint air
like an unnumbered galaxy—

for the ruptured self
to disappear.

Pieces
for L

On Valentine's, florists
hire extras: arrangers,
roses, deliverers of cupids
with hearts pinned to boxes—
their false messages
ride in vans, are hoisted
by Fabio-impersonators into cars,
adulterer's apartments,
the hands of singles
aching to wear rings.
On Valentine's, one
thirty-something remains
an observer. No roses arrive,
no Chippendale's hunks
appear at her door;
only a valentine,
meanly given,
fires past her face,
flies like a missing piece
into the crease of her own
valentine lying on the floor.
The woman has always
hated puzzles,
their mystery shapes,
lopped-off fronds
of bedroom pillows,
broken window ledges,
tongues belonging
to questioning mouths,
where is my other,
where is my fit?

She will find those
orphaned valentines
and reach for scissors.
She will cut their bodies
into a mound of confetti.
She will rip until the woman
and her lover lie still within
a jigsaw of paper drift,
a shredder's delight,
a torturer's safehouse.
They'll touch through hundreds
of dropped petals,
the crinkly wrapping
of cellophane.
Yes, cupid has pierced them
with his little naughty,
the whole city feels it.
Their bare skins punctured,
she bursts into bloom
when he enters her,
the liquid of his sex spraying
like uncorked champagne.
Hey, isn't it time
the delivery man arrived?

Him

I'm far enough away to make this possible:
rearrange opinions of him like furniture.
Compare the violet lining around
the pupils of his eyes

to the bedcover in that motel. The one
where he put the quarter in
to make the bed shake without
having to do anything.

He had excuses each time
for meeting me except
real ones: a drink, quick fuck.
Hoping I wouldn't notice how much

he talked about his mother's hair
once being my color. Red
as a whore's dress; as sky
exhaling over us, lung tissue.

In February looking up and out
the window of a '60 Chevy
and wondering when the glow
was going to start.

Remembering's easy as
knocking over a table
or chair. When I stick
my nose in an old car

I hear our words
mingling like down
falling out of a pillow.
"Did you see it, that red spark

over the hill?" The comet Kohoutek
practically invisible
was his last excuse for driving
to an unfinished highway

in the middle of a Texas prairie.
For a sight that was supposed
to rivet me to another galaxy.
That's when the glow started

and I didn't have to fumble
with the divider in the front seat
or comb my hair or even
put the quarter in.

Carla Hartsfield

Oullette Avenue, Windsor

The evening, hot
and sanding across
skin like sawdust,
starts to rise,
forms invisible poles
and stay-strings, the sky
angular as a circus tent.
And the performers,
painted and costumed,
step from hotels
surrounding water,
somehow know
that the crowd
is waiting, longs
to see them bare
enormous bellies no
T-shirt could cover,
or Popeye muscles
and sculpted thighs;
the crowd turns
sequinned eyes
on the casino shuttle
that brought them here
for the pre-gambling
peep show—blink
at multiple suns

fizzling out of
Labatt's Blue cups,
even as they raise them
to the light and observe
a metaphysical splitting
of carbonated atoms—
witness a bride and groom
playing the slots
before hitting the sack.
They all must have this.
But, what of the
psychopath with his
winning smiles
and darting eyes,
the young woman he
follows home after losing
his credit card advance
at a Black Jack table?
The woman has already
noticed him and flags down
a cop. The bride takes
the plastic casino tub
with a hundred fake coins
and cashes them in.
The circus tent darkens
and tightly-dressed
performers look naked

as they coax the crowd
out with them along
spotlit sidewalks.
Inside the casino,
regulars want a show
and customers
line up. Money carts
jostle down aisles like
stretch limos, ringing
their cylinders of
solidified tears.
Some scenarios demand
perfection. *Listen.*
If you stand still enough
you can hear the key
to the psychopath's mind
clicking this way
and that. It's the sound
of a missing conscience,
a mix of greed and desire,
of the teeth in the
groom's zipper being ripped
and spilt one by one
onto the casino floor, because
the bride was willing.

Wildcat

Oh, those sweltering, summer nights when you shimmied yourself out of the local car wash and went for a reckless spin on gravel roads, the couples who necked in your windows, the stars you saw tumbling into the lake from the top of Lonely Heart Trail with its wicked curves and even wickede*r* rock surfaces cupped under your white, leather lap, your chrome-covered ass. Oh, the rattle-snake belts and lizard-skin boots you've endured, the bullhorn that bellowed "The Eyes Of Texas," the perfumed scarves, the twisters, the lightning, the moonshine. And now you've pulled up to a liquor store in southern Ontario and a Truman Capote look-alike wearing a big, straw Stetson has stepped from your vintage figure, a cat's tail swinging from your rearview mirror. Oh, to do something really wild like drive yourself off a cliff, refuse to start, refuse to be a 1967 Buick Wildcat, a quick fix for convertible aficionados; refuse to be driven, to coat yourself in red, to parade down any old street just for the hell of it; refuse to let your doors swing open and shut in perfect rhythm for hungry lovers, refuse to be sexy *just once.*

Rising
for Bronwen Wallace

Glittering stem of light
inside the window. Four a.m.
and whiteness pours
into a lone figure, her
sheer-gowned body filled.

She's gone in seconds—
hypnotically, that form
shimmering in place
of her life
wants to tell
every secret;
river called night
drinks the moon.

Eventually, there was
nothing to do except
rise unconsciously
embracing black water,
the stars
erupting as usual.

Pierre L'Abbé

Pierre L'Abbé has published fiction as well as non-fiction on the topics of politics and art. He is a former poetry editor of *Scrivener*, a McGill literary journal, and a former co-ordinator of the Phoenix Poetry Workshop. In January 1996, he became host of the ART BAR, Toronto's largest poetry reading series. He is a Policy Advisor with the Ministry of Municipal Affairs and Housing with responsibility for environmental co-ordination. He holds a Ph.D. in comparative religion from the University of Toronto and now lives in Toronto with his wife and three children.

Song, After Leonard Cohen

when your head lies diagonal
like a sash
I can read in your sad eyes
subtitles

in a language written
by pigeons in concrete
a transcription of the scream of gulls
searching eggs
blown from sky-scrapers

beyond you in the darkness
a cat slinks
across my roof
when I approach
you turn your back

through barbed wire
I can see your heart
emaciated
feeding the birds

Pierre L 'Abbé

Your Red Lips

in pale light
my tongue
traces fingers
to your nails
unpainted

against my
disappointment
you recoil
like Mary from
the scroll and lily
of Gabriel

to hold my
desire
you offer me
glossy red lips
to abraise
and bite

when all your paint
is licked off
my lips grow
restless
over your waist,
round hips

in the sudden retreat
of your knees
I read a fear
of my fetish for
red toe nails

if I find
plain white toes
what will you offer
my lips
that is deep red
to console them
this time

Fallen Novel

When I reached 42nd Street
You plunged 27 stories
out of my memory
I was not sure if you stopped
a month short
of hitting the pavement
and though my forever
being uncertain
will be a tick in dog fur
behind my ear
I'll still sing the love song

Louella held me
"I'm so tight"

On a lonely evening
sniffing the swap of faces
on the Boulevard des Italiens
I didn't expect to see you
falling
from a Japanese bank
but I knew you hit this time
from the subtle change
in the hum of the crowd
Sitting in a packed café
I wonder why one woman
surreptitiously looks
at the legs of another
and with my chin in my hand
I watch the street sweeper
clean up your long, long body
and pass over half the head
and a sidewalk artist's
pastel earless Van Gogh
but the mouth is still singing

Louella held me
"I'm so tight"

For the longest time
I didn't know
it was you
sitting on top of Lord Nelson
in the middle of Trafalgar Square
When you stood so graciously
to dive from the column
I hesitated for a moment
to turn you in
but you jumped with a smile
naked, you hit
your arms and legs spread
You are Trafalgar Square
and I have walked every stone
chanting
"It's mine, they can't have it."

But they had it
A few months later
they returned you to me
I keep you in a narrow box, somewhere
I run across you
whenever I move
and think next time
I'll open the box
I hesitate to repack you
and hold the box
in my hand a moment
I see you falling
and sing to myself

Louella held me
"I'm so tight"

Pierre L'Abbé

At the mantle

At the mantle, men's elbows between vases: a discussion on the bedroom behaviour of our coochee hostess.

Children scramble in the antechamber and I wonder why they care to initiate me into this circle—

At the dinner table polite inquires as to my activities. Through the silence of the mastications, I describe a day of caring for my baby and forays to the libraries.

The hostess accepts compliments on the food, explains that she is half French and half Canadian but really more French, and this emphasis explains the accents of the cuisine while whispers circle around the mismatched candles that all the food came prepared from the *charcuterie*.

Coochee asks me if I plan to stay home and raise my daughter for the rest of my life.

I search the faces for a rebuttal from elsewhere, but find a matrix of eyes skewed toward me, an orchestra of poised forks.

In the library

In the library, J tells me he found his mother crying. A friend committed suicide, she had attempted many times. Last week, after leaving a dinner party with old school mates, she jumped into the Rhône.

The body was just found. She had been very "up" at dinner. Her friends wanted to drive her home. She walked.

J says that meant she had decided, this was not an attempt, not another call for help.

I think of this story for days. One question I cannot stop repeating: Why the Rhône? The Rhône is so impersonal. It is wide, shores are flat. The Saône is swifter, but gentler. The Rhône is a man. The Saône is androgynous, it talks to all its visitors, gently coercing, like Satan. The Rhône is indifferent, treats you like just another pesky soul who wants to jump in for a free ride to another world.

How could this woman choose the Rhône?

Pierre L'Abbé

from Bourgeois Angels

through her smoke of my disintegrating vision
I lurch for
the shift of skirts on hips
the creases on the backs of jackets
the light of leaves

hounding the scent of citron
I press the wind
moulding dresses into bodies
blowing men into air

while dodging the flight of pebbles
I throw myself after the clip of trouser cuffs
the silent tip tap of the hem
of a short knit skirt

I know an absence

I know an absence that would not tolerate taking its leave while I slept.

A dream hangs heavy on the edge of my consciousness. I restart the player, again and again, but the dismalness of the irretrievable dream sits like the tightness of a peaked cap drawn over my brow.

Sleep has come to me again, bartering through my unwilling eyes. I heard the echo of his ugly laughter as he escaped without paying; he will return in sixteen hours, pomegranate in hand.

Awake now, I know, I use the energy of day, draw my face close to the mirror: one profile gives way to the consideration of the other. Neither side will accept my reflection. I part my hair on the wrong side.

Shivering and hunched, I listen to my jeans clip to the press stand for the American paper. Wakefulness has made a sports fan of me. In the café with café crème, I live a half hour on baseball figures.

Anger swells in my loins on the pulse of each step. It's not passion I feel, but the surge of the Saône in my groin.

Sitting by the river, my feet over, I am lost in my reflection being dragged away by water. Each time it gently bobs, I reel it back. Sleepy, I rest my head against the pier of the Passerelle St Georges. Perhaps I've been awake before.

Lies

are in touch
with reality getting out of hand

in the hand of Anna as Freud

gave up on truth for lies

between the sheets
that rode the humidity on his breath when it hit her skin and
he said

"The existentialists don't have the courage to look."

-s a man has as he stabs his own hand
and sings with Louis

what a wonderful world
this could be without all those people lying

around in Heaven, singing I'm in heaven

or I must be if Ella and Louis are smiling
at Richard's nix on the truth when he said:

"I lied to the American people."

believing finally there will be no more lying

on a couch getting counselling to cope

-ing is a remedy for truth

is only found when Louis blows that long long note

how I can lie
with you

Alexandra Leggat

Alexandra Leggat is a poet and freelance writer living in Toronto. She studied Magazine Journalism at Ryerson Polytechnic University and her reviews, interviews and articles have appeared in various magazines. She has dabbled in television, music and theatre, has travelled extensively, and lived in more places than she cares to mention. Poetry, books and dogs are a few of her favourite things. It is a love of words and writing that feeds her life, and the unpredictable nature of life itself that feeds her writing. Her poetry has been published in *Ink* magazine, *McGill Street, Zygote, paperplates, Symposium* and *Oh!* Magazine.

Cropped Up in San Francisco

when I knew you last
your golden baby hair
swayed like my breezy thoughts about you
and the great life you were leading
south of the border

sun-kissed skin's a far cry
from the rice and bean-curd complexion
that's stretched across your hairless head
and slouching in front of me at our point of reunion—
this is what Zen has done for you?

your California crazed-up fantasies
can only be cashed in in L.A.
you say
and you lead me to your one-eyed girlfriend
who's been baking bread since 5 a.m.
and just informed you she's pregnant and happy
about it

I play Pacman in the cafe
at the end of Haight Street
and think about Seal Rock
and Alcatraz
eating jelly beans
one for each of life's little religions.
You're somewhere else
on your knees with your eyes closed

Like Bugs

Some days I feel like I'm sitting in a city alley
catching flies on my tongue
tapping my foot to an old song
trying to drown out a nagging thought
that's buzzing around my head like flies

> and *I wish I could sense danger*
> *like an animal*
> *and run like anger*
> *when a bottle becomes a blanket*

I have a Marc Bolan fear of cars
of anything too futile and metallic
that could drive me to my grave,
of porcelain boys who'll break me
to keep themselves unscathed

> and *I wish I could sense danger*
> *like an animal*
> *and run like anger*
> *when a bottle becomes a blanket*

I wonder why a thing like God is strange to me
I wouldn't know it if I tripped over it
and I wish that I would
that I could
catch it on my tongue
like a bug

Providence

here I stand, so close to young
yet years away from when it all began

no matter how I change
these little-girl-untamed-eyes won't close

and all my reflecting
fails to enlighten me

I'm unable to continue
without resolving where I've come from

but how many times can I go back
before I'm swallowed by my past

do I have to take this
right back to the womb

sorry Mum, I should have called
I know you weren't expecting to be expecting me again

Alexandra Leggat

Ton Of Bricks

And if tired is the end
then I'm ending
heavy-lidded

loaded
like I'd swallowed a hundred bullets
and shot my mouth off

all I've got to show for it is tired

body heavy—an elephant's
a hundred me's could fit into an elephant
but an elephant has fit into me

I lumber to bed
and fall into sleep

five minutes it seems
and the next day is knocking pestilently
on my skull

but I'm not ready for more
I'm not ready

and if it were easy
I'd be dead—
but I'm dead tired

it's the best I can do

Radiate Her

The radiator never stops pounding
the heart stops pounding
where's the justice in that
why don't we get to choose our own plumbing

I want to be warm like a radiator
I don't care if I bang and creak
if I have to be bled to give off heat

I just want to be sturdy
and exude warmth

Alexandra Leggat

Who is who

to find you
behind the guttural comings and goings of a winter thaw

you, choking
on an abiding sense of your self
that caught in your throat on its way up to blossom

habitually, I save you
and into the depths that you intended to surface
I submerge

we contend with the fight for breath

I catch mine first

I always do

Lost (Be)cause

feel this, this not knowing
this reaching inside of yourself
and finding that everything you were
is gone
and it's a mystery
when you left
where you went

you're hoping that you're just hiding
gathered yourself into a pile
and shoved yourself
every little bit of yourself
behind a shoulder blade
a stomach muscle
your spleen

you wish you could go back
back to when your tongue began speaking words
you didn't think it knew
when your eyes began seeing things
that weren't even there
and all the other trips
you're mind's taking you through

where on earth were you
when you slipped away
maybe you were sleeping
that's when it most likely happened
so you go back to sleep
and hope for your return
you sleep and you sleep
dreaming that maybe
come springtime
you'll just grow back

Alexandra Leggat

Trailer Parks And Gurus

Trailer parks and Gurus line the I-90 like embroidery
on a linen dish cloth
but not as decorative
the trailer parks are visible the gurus are not
but they're there, somewhere, in between the lines
making history
literary, musical, political and on and on kind of history

America has a backward further ahead kind-of-ness
an openness in a blind sort of way
like twin peaks

it's a different hue
the skies an off-white and the people hazy,
it's Hollywood and Chicago
gangsters, moviestars
poets and bohemia
it's Milwaukee and Idaho
beer and potatoes
it's Montana and New Mexico
and forty eight other things

a capitalist charisma
in proletariat shoes

a catalyst

a non-sequitur

Steve McCabe

Steve McCabe is a visual artist and poet. He is the author/ illustrator of *Wyatt Earp in Dallas: 1963* (Seraphim Editions 1995).

He dropped out of high school and travelled with a psychedelic tent show in a carnival, selling tickets and reading poetry. When Uncle Sam drafted him for the war in Vietnam, he moved to Canada.

He is also an art instructor and the creator of children's imagination activity features published by the Toronto Star. He has appeared at The Word on The Street festival in Toronto, leading children and their families in creating poetry together.

Steve has painted murals, exhibited works on paper, and been an Artist in Residence at Artpark (Lewiston, N.Y.).

A Man Like Me

You hiccup below your belly.
A bullet hits me.
I bring you chocolate and flowers.
Wine trickles out of my mouth.

I'm a goat. You're a woman.
Licking you on all fours.

Jesus in the corner.
Nobody knows the real story.
He's not gonna tell me.

Gives me a thorn.
Bite it when the pain's too great.

Disappears like lava going back to the volcano.
What I'm doing must be okay.

You fill my mouth.
I pass it back to you.
We touch each other's face.

A man like me can be happy.

It's a mind body thing.
Love is a bullet.
It's got to come out.

The Knuckles of a Killer

Inside the tent at the front of the line
I look at a hand.

The fingernails are cut but the knuckles
are terrifying and that's what I've paid
to touch.

When the hand twitches I lean away.
Somebody outside yells, "What's taking all day?"

Killing stains the present tense
by erasing yesterday and tomorrow.
That's what's taking all day.

In the eerie glow of kerosene light
I look at my palm.
Why should I worry about my lifeline?
This is entertainment.

Did he kill his children? His wife?
Beat a man to death?

Maybe on a motorcycle
he was the right side of the law,
the cop tracking Bonnie and Clyde,
pumping machine gun bullets
into their bisexual tunnel of love.

The hand moves slightly in the deepening shadows.
How much of a cut does he get from this?

A voice outside yells, "Somebody die in there or what?"

I make my hand into a fist
upside down rub my knuckles against his
slowly bumping bone to bone
until it pulls behind black cloth hanging down.
"Times up," says a bald guy holding a handkerchief.
"I used to be a coroner," he tells me.

We watch the hand reappear.

He spits on it.
The hand lunges like an alligator.

I'm in the shadows.
A little story runs through my head.
The hand is covered in blood.
It fires a gun.
It grips the bars of a jail cell.
It wants to wash a woman's face.

I step into the sunshine.

The knuckles on my right hand grow heavy.

Coal

People say I look like him.
How he looked his first day back.

He couldn't stay away.
It was us on every channel in his brain.
The way our skin turned white when we slept
pushed up against the pink of our lips,
speckled with coal dust
smeared by his invisible fingers.

He couldn't stay away.
We were radio waves
defrosting the North Pole where his plane went down.

He made a final charge for the magnetic
fields
which bubbled in our mouths.

He typed late at night on a piece of black felt.
The temperature set higher than his furnace could take.

The Prehistoric Films of India

They knew how to create
a box of fire
while inside
hands of ash clapped in paradise.

On Tour

Dwayne Eddy's guitar filled the air,
and my fingers touched her tomato soup mouth.

She gerbilled herself into my arms
and I lockjawed her with my passion-ivity,
loving every minute.

Wasting every day,
on tour with Dwayne Eddy.

Striking deep into your tomato soup zone,
giving you lots of electric strings.

Steve McCabe

Adding to the Book

A loner from the west
well-versed in electronic scriptures
sends his pick-up truck on a sacred mission
via remote control
from his perch on the porch.

The wife peels potatoes,
his children play kickball,
and the neighbours attend
an Aryan Nation Revival.

His loneliness is blessed and wonderful.

A hawk circles the children.

It's a wonder that a man so remote and driven
can leave the fingerprints of human frailty
as a testimony to cursive writing.

Beneath the windshield wiper
is his addendum to the Book of Revelations
explaining timers, black powder, and nails

focused ostensibly on the birth of a child
enlarged to include the demise of creation
sold at the local hardware store

to a man fiddling with an electronic box
not concerned with a hawk dropping down
as steam rises from potatoes
and the neighbours who expelled him
watch his truck roll into the compound.

He watches from a hill
at peace with his divinely ordered unfolding
not hearing the shouts
as talons grip his youngest child
and smoke rises to God.

Three wise men—college boys really—
discover the bones of a child on the mountain
after identifying wildflowers.

They recall a newspaper story.
And offer delicate petals
as gifts to the child.

They transmit sacred information
about the day's discoveries
via lap top computer.

Sitting on her porch
the wife peels potatoes
watching her kids play kickball
and preparing for the drive
on visiting day.

She does not believe that he has added
to the Book of Revelations.

She believes her baby was lost to misfortune.

She is as rooted in the earth
as wildflowers in mountain soil.

She isn't interested in electronics.

Which is why she will drive the truck herself.

Monuments

Unmarked monuments drift with the fog
that fills my chest.
Never in my wildest dreams of sober clarity
did I imagine such weightlessness possible.
As your tears evaporate mine turn into the flood.
I smell judgement like rotting fish
as they publicly enter your private space.

Tonight you will grieve with others who beat their
chests and check their wristwatches,
but not for what we have lost.
Tonight is scheduled for innocence elsewhere.

In spite of the blowing fog stinking up my chest I get hard
for what's between those legs.
But my point is—
and I still don't think you get it,
you kissed an unfinished monument that tonight's
audience would call rubble.

Tonight you will grieve with others
so selective I am infuriated, barely stopping myself.

Walking in a park I find myself followed by
an unfinished monument,
moving rubble some say.
I want to shovel stones over you
and see you howling like the women of Teheran,
but you are as selective as the colour wheel.

I believe that if you bury grief it will eat you alive,
but this grief is eating me from the ankles up.
I can't walk to the park, those damned statues
have gotten inside me.
I hear them howling, stinking as they rot
and driving me mad.
How dare you commemorate the innocents struck down
elsewhere.
I'm sorry about the others, but listen to me
those people tonight impersonating the women of Teheran
have holes in their chest.
Listen to the wind.
Don't tell me those zigzagging whispers
bouncing off corners
trapped inside a cyclone is compassion
that binds you to them.
If you do, you'll prove to me that your colour wheel
is at the bottom of the ocean,
thrown away selectively.

Oregon Trail Shoulders

She soaps the soles of my feet.
I lift one knee like a stag.
She massages my ankle, shin, calf.
Tells me to put my foot down.
Repeats the process.

Her fingers move into my face,
erasing shadows with white foam.
The near boiling water on my neck
relaxes my Oregon Trail shoulders.
Eddies of current cross my thighs.
She takes me in her mouth.
Tells me I am finished. We trade places.

I part her jet black hair with loosened fingers.
She is beneath a volcanic waterfall.
I wipe soap off her forehead and nose.

In my other life, wagons roll past fields of tall grass.
In the dry season, lightning storms set this swaying ocean
on fire.
She is lightning and the rain that follows.
Cooking me potatoes with coriander and green onion.

Gary McCarty

For Jackie,

My friend and
fellow lover of
words, and more —
of language.

Alan

05/12/96

Gary McCarty was born in Brooklyn, New York, and raised on Long Island. Educated at St. Norbert College in DePere, Wisconsin, Gary moved with his wife to Toronto in 1975. A career banker, he has been writing full time for the past year, and is presently working on a novel and editing a collection of his short fiction. He lives in Whitby, Ontario.

God's Breath

Fog outside the window, opaque,
God's icy breath,
rolls in,
leaves moisture
on the warm glass.

I stand over
my mother,
comatose
under white sheets.

Plastic umbilici
sprout from her body
like sea grass rooted in
undulating sand dunes,
green ocean foaming, the rising
tide extending its reach.

Sea birds gather, calling
in anger,
hunger to mate,
to feed, always
wanting
more,

never satisfied,

like death.

Gary McCarty

Medicine Man

In the dream
white coated doctors,
copper faces painted half
red, half blue, overlaid with moons
and stars,
dance in circles around
my mother's bed,

invoking
the Four Directions.

Gritty smoke
of burning sage passes across
her body, like small clouds of dust
raised by hooves
of galloping ponies.

Fields of tall grasses, rippling
in the wind to the edge
of the horizon, fill the dream, surrounding
the bed of my sleeping mother.

I wake
to the hum of machines
recording the signs of her life,
the banality of the chrome and sterile white
room broken only by splashes of chrysanthemums
and violets.

I lean over my mother, wipe sweat from her forehead, run
my fingers through her matted hair, rub smooth
the skin of her cork screw cheeks.

Her toothless mouth surrounds
a breathing tube—
wanting always
the things of life.

Gary McCarty

Left Standing

I stand
naked
before her.

She sits
on the bed's edge,
glances up
to catch my eye.

She lifts her nightshirt
briefly,
then releases it to gravity.

Rising, she looks away and
moves past me,
politely excusing herself
on her way
downstairs
to the kitchen.

Laying Claim

I am surprised
by the little girl giggle
bubbling from my new lover's throat.

The tender spot on her neck
touched with a fleeting pass of my lips
as her fingers danced with mine
is claimed by me;

I found the place.

The rest of her is hers;
it is this spot I want.

And I will return to it
when there is a need, whether the need
be hers or mine.

Gary McCarty

Markings

I drive the spade
into soil,
working in rhythm
with some internal clock.

My ten year old boy stands
between the split earth
and the glaring sun.

He is
a mass of undefined features,
light grinning at his edges.

His shadow falls into my hole,
bending to conform
to its angular space.

Rocks and dirt
shoveled onto the pile, land with
small thuds, like mortar shells
impacting in the distance.

Through six trips
emptying the wheelbarrow,
my white-haired boy holds his place,

silently watching
the cavity take shape, from a ragged wound
spotted with orange clay—
like my son at his birth,
splattered with red, viscous shrapnel,
the mark of expulsion from
his mother's womb—
to become a round, sloping hole,
dug deeply enough
to root its tree.

Gary McCarty

Conversations With My Brother

You've left, I know,
but I have
your bones. They
stand on a shelf in my house.
I talk to you there.
A piece of you
hangs from my neck.

I celebrated
your birthday last month
with Cotts cream soda and home made
chocolate cake,
like when we were kids.

And Thomas, I want
to tell you Mom spoke
of you this Mother's Day, her first mention
of your name
since
that scotch and phenobarbital
cocktail put you to sleep
during a late night
television movie.

There's not much else—you know
how it seems
to pour
when it rains? Lately, it's been
dry
as bone.

Nacia Miller

Nacia Miller was born in Brooklyn, New York in 1948. In university she studied both music and art history, graduating in 1971 from Hunter College in Manhattan with a BA in art history.

After graduation Nacia worked in video production and public access cable television in Rochester, New York and in Louisville, Kentucky. Later, she worked in public relations for not-for-profit and private sector companies in the U.S. and in Canada, where she moved in 1979. Since 1989 she has worked full time as a freelance writer.

Nacia has been writing poetry and short stories for the past eight years, and her work has appeared in *Blood + Aphorisms; nepenthe Poetry WLU;* and in the U.S. poetry journal *Poetpourri.* She lives in Toronto with her husband Marc, their son Aaron, and dog Jenny.

Mother Love

I went down to the cellar
to find you,
only child
ripping and tearing up the place
possessed and oblivious and brave and mad
to watch you,
in wonder, raw torment

Down to the cellar
where you've always been
infant, toddler, schoolboy,
man-child now
riffing on your electric guitar
shooting hoops
out of the damp darkness
while I memorize your swagger,
nailbitten fingers on metal strings,
turnaround jump shot
down to the cellar
way past fear
where loss grows its mushroom life

This can't be love
this terror

I hear your voice

I hear your voice
cutting through the madness
of the clicking cicadas
on a hot summer evening
Soon the fireflies will show themselves again.

In your powder-blue housecoat
with the scalloped sleeves
and the peter pan collar
you hold open the kitchen door
with one hand
and lean out into the summers of my life
one more time.

"You wanna cuppa coffee?"

The sound reaches me
across the paved driveway
over the parked station wagon
through the pattern of silver grey cyclone fence
the abandoned bicycle
a barking dog
a crying grandchild

The metal clang of the gate closing
forever.

I call back to you
through the silent dusk
Yes
and thank you so much
for asking.

Inside silence

I have a clean, tidy house
in drawers the spoons are neatly stacked
according to size and shape
my corners are free of dust
and the floors shine with a polish
I apply while on my knees
and still at night the crystal patterns explode
on the surface of my eyelids
light the path through my pristine hallways
point the way out the back door
into the tangle
homeland, garden

The suicides have come to visit

The suicides have come to visit.
They sit in repeating progression
Multiple exposures on my rocking chair
Five angels who make no sudden moves
Forlorn, disgraced, content
They mean to stay the night.

The two shooting stars are healed now
Finished with bloody razors and shotgun shells.
They rock, they smile through closed lips
The beautiful blond boy
As ripped and patched and frayed as his own thin clothing.
And the other, wrapped in dark wool
Sick with illness he could not bear.
They pecked out their pitiful goodbyes
begged to be held, but it was a nasty trick
You know, you never know
the hideous secrets.

And grandfather in his black top coat
Full-lipped and stern as in the ancient portrait
Looking at something lost in the distance
Remote, posing: Let them remember me this way.
He put the cat out and some milk in a saucer
And he turned on the gas.

Then the two shimmering women
Light reflecting baggage
who laugh out loud while making no sound
Lipstick red, cigarette dangling
Sexually urgent, eternal yearning
They know me best.
Before they turned on the gas
They put the children out, and some cookies with the milk.

The suicides are on the landing.
Grandfather glances up as I move slowly downstairs
He leans to let me pass.
The boys are very clean
They bear no trace of bloodbath
or massive wound
or wrenching grimacing parting with I am
They offer only their exquisite choosing.
The women are fiercely beautiful
They don't smell of sweat or tobacco
They take up too much space
and yet they don't get in the way.

The suicides have come to stay.
Stilled lives gathered round the piano
Glazed, protected, past, over, complete,
stopped before it gets
rather late in the day
and re-evaluation becomes necessary.

Nacia Miller

Wedding Album

The one in this picture looks surprised,
caught on her special day
trying to get out
of a rented limousine, one hoof on the pavement,
one stuck in the gown's satin folds
holding fast to a trembling bouquet of fresh
hay and baby's breath, she works to maintain
her balance, concerned that perhaps her veil
may have slipped.

The one in this picture recovers in time
for the next shot, with china and silverware
previously selected, she trots with purpose
out of the limo and into the corral,
remembers her vows and does not bare her teeth
when required to lift
her skirt for the garter toss.

Your Affair

Last night, you said you felt dangerous.
Yearning to touch the sky, and
the heat of our desperate desire
you said I was so beautiful,
I felt your fingers tremble as they brushed
the tears, the clouds
that shuddered on the surface of our skin.

This morning, you have a different opinion
of our shadowy flight.
As the sun shines through the trees
and the panes of my glass house,
I listen as you weep your
sick, sad sack of sin
and shame,
shame on us.

Tomorrow, tomorrow
afloat on a fitful star
I'll measure the weight of this disaster
against the sound of your car door
exploding the sweet void.

Nacia Miller

Borrowed Book

I wish I
still had that book
I lent it to a friend, gone

lent it to him with casual ease,
forgetting future reference,
                              remembrance

when I saw him for the first time
I trembled with electric shock
        he stood soft in a crowded room
        of metal-edged need and I,
        silk scarved hunger hidden,
        knew him

never mind, my point is, how
to get the book back?

I know what you're thinking
        but I can't get another
        can't find it anywhere
        believe me, I've tried

the problem is,
he has the only book in the world
indelibly inscribed
                        mine, mine

Nedra

Arun Rodrigo who writes as Nedra, is a freelance journalist who writes post-colonial fiction and poetry that draw from her experiences as a political refugee. She would write even more if she didn't live with four cats who demand to be waited on paw and foot.

She uses her poems as photographs to capture a memory, so it has not yet ceased to amaze her that others find something in them to relate to. She still believes in fundamental human decency, so she would like to think that her perspective will help contribute to tolerance, through understanding.

Iruthayammal

Life wove its way through her face
leaving behind labyrinths
her features travelled
carrying her every expression.

Her voice was a cradle
that dipped me into an ocean of stars;
and drew me back gurgling
to brush away fronds of seaweed
from my forehead.

Close to her heart she held me
and my spirit nourished—would
stir thoughts into words that I
tasted and spat out to her applause.

She gave me the moon, ripe and smooth
as my mother's womb—and fed me
jasmines and curd, stroking my child-bones
so I would grow strong.

She frightened demons away with incense
and disease with burning
margosa leaves—she would draw the very
plague from my body; and purge it
with trembling hands.

My grandmother is small,
wrinkled as a raisin, dried in the Indian sun
nervous and frenetic—she is yet the goddess
of content homes and soothed children.

The Matchmaker Aunts

"But she's so dark!"
The matchmaker aunts swooping in
like a flock of overfed magpies,
to pass judgement on my marriageability,
and I just ten years old at the time.

My father growled in defence:
brown, brown, a true South Indian
golden brown, the brown of sun and soil.
But what did he know of brownness,
he was fair-skinned.
My mother too, like my grandfather—
who was often mistaken for an Englishman.

They swooned over my cousins
the matchmaker aunts
"No trouble finding a match for this one."
Fair-skinned, dimpled, fragile beauties.
And my grandmother, darker than I
would throw up her hands
and scurry away to her kitchen
in exasperation.

I was the duckling fated
never to reach swanhood.

In later years I would hear with disbelief
the flattery of men, and sometimes women.
Having no claim to transient beauty
nothing to fall back on
except my own strength—I learned
to walk straighter, to look men
in the eye.
I had no bashful beauty to hide
from the lecherous eyes of deceivers.

But aunts, dear aunts!
those who behold my skin
speak not of its darkness, but smooth,
how smooth it is, and soft.
I am not fragile, but they marvel at
the strength of my arms,
and how straight my back, the curve
of my waist, the flare of my hips.

And yes, I have not met my match!

And aunts, dear aunts!
I thank you for the gift
you threw me—a scrap over your shoulder
on leaving my grandfather's house.
You were my fairy godmothers
proclaiming with gracious condescension
as you shuffled at the door:
"Well, at least she's intelligent."

The child who is not mine

The child who is not mine
was born... well what does it
matter when? she was born
in the same hospital I was born in
delivered by the same gynaecologist
choked, gasped, gurgled, spat and screamed
in the same operating theatre

She was born in the afternoon
while I was away at school
and when I saw her I wept:

I was no longer an only daughter
she was so small and pink and wrinkled
she needed me—human spool
(If I touched her I could feel the warmth
of the chrysalis from which I'd crawled out once)
mostly because she had claimed me
and I would be hers and not she mine

When I held out my hands
the women in crisp-starched white
shook their heads

I wonder if they were afraid she might taste
the tears that dropped on her face
and screaming crawl back to
that safe warm place where
life does not taste salt-bitter-sweet

bomb explodes

bomb explodes
somewhere in the distance
like a single cannon fired
and a hundred people cease to exist
no more for them the laughing-talking-
eating-belching-farting-fornicating
vulgar bliss that is life
only sleep
In her room a girl
wonders
if—there is a moment of epiphany
    between the boom! body hurtling
    and the shock (oh dear god!) falling
if—the mind can tear itself away from
    searing flesh and regret to
    suddenly grasp at harmony
if—it is a sin to be glad (so sweetly glad)
    that the bomb sounds so far away
    and sanctuary can be sought
    in
    a

    pillow

In the House of Green Shadows

In the house of green shadows
its walls enclose her like a tomb
and she remembers a sarcophagus
of another time.
Deprived of light her skin
has turned to parchment.

>   Deprived of hope her soul
>   has turned to ashes.
>   Imprisoned in an attic
>   by a riotous mob
>   in a silence marred by
>   explosions that sound a little
>   too close, she watches
>   through barred windows
>   her childhood crumble
>   like the landmarks turned
>   to rubble in the zeal of
>   fresh bubbling hatred.
>   There is a smell of burning
>   flesh that permeates
>   everything now, her clothes
>   reek of its cloying incense and
>   the smell of blood when she
>   menstruates—nauseates her. She
>   claws at her belly sometimes, the
>   deaths inside her make her ill
>   and she must expel it forever
>   or herself
>   die.

In the new country
where she adds to the
statistics of immigrants
the silence of the house
is broken by her friends.
They ask her questions
sometimes—she answers
curtly.
She knows they are offended.
They want theatrics—these
untouched people.
She turns away in disdain,
she will not have her
tranquillity
broken by their
disgust.

Star walker

I remember some nights—when
serenaded by an orchestra of grasshoppers

I would lie on my back on
a hard wooden bench

the bench had been used by the family for years
made by my grandfather in his backyard

it supported my child-body with
the unchanging sturdiness of love-labour

and a plethora of nicks and scratches
like a family portrait

I was Queen with a sleeping dog on either
side guarding me from night-creatures

on these nights I would stare
at the sky, and lifting my legs perpendicular

to the ground, slowly step onto the stars
my body—often earthbound would

release itself gradually, and I would float
with the universe at my feet—until

I was pulled back to earth by the
overpowering fragrance of araliya

or my mother's fried-fish curry tugging
at my belly from the other side of the house

In time
these nights became less frequent

but I didn't mind—so much my brain
overflowed with a constellation of words

gravity, relativity, ontology, phenomenology
to those who taught me

I tried to bring my own galaxies unfurling
I told them I could walk on stars

they smiled—
this is what they do when they can't think what to say

when they did speak—what you say you step on
may be light from a long dead star—

it was only to tell me such things
are impossible

through a thickening mist
i assure them

indeed it is possible, it is, it is!
it is just that i have forgot how

Woman Eating a Peach

It doesn't matter to him that the
world continues it's revolution—he
must stop and stare at
the woman eating a peach.

In her hands at first
the peach reposes—fruit of temptation.

She gently wipes it clean
with a corner of her pristine T-shirt.
She smells it, eyes closed inhaling deeply
and then bites into it.
Her teeth sink into fuzzy skin
and sunset flesh,
dribbling juice from the sides of her puckered lips,
she sucks it back in with
an almost laugh.
She has discovered an oasis in the
middle of a sweltering traffic-jam.
Now her eyes sparkle
as the peach rotates in the hold of
her fingers, and a slender river flows
into the gorge of her palm
and down her wrist.
With artful delicacy
she devours embodied voluptuousness
and finally leans back in her seat.
The fruit now reduced to a wrinkled head
she casts it away.

He is aware that he is caught in
a rush of activity—but
for some minutes he is uncertain
what to do.

Acknowledgements

Ronna Bloom

Several of these poems have been published previously: "Blue Raft" and "This Clean" in The *Canadian Forum*; "Landlady" in *The Antigonish Review*.

"Blue Raft," "This Clean," "Landlady" and "The Job of an Apple" will appear in the collection, *Fear of the Ride*, to be published in 1996 by Harbinger Poetry Series at Carleton University Press.

Robert Boates

Some poems have been published previously in *Hamilton Haiku Press*, *paperplates* and *Cactus Tree Press*.

Afua Cooper

"Womanhood," "The Power of Racism," and "And I Remember" were previously published in *Memories Have Tongue*, Sister Vision, 1992.

Nancy Dembowski

"Autumn's Surrender" first appeared as a chapbook by Tortoiseshell and Black Press. "You'll Never Get Them Both In Bed," and "It Wasn't Until Later" have all appeared in *Oversion* Magazine. "Sweets" has appeared in both *SinOverTan* Magazine and the *Word Up* CD.

Alexandra Leggat

"Trailer Parks and Gurus" appeared in *Ink* Magazine, Spring/Summer 1995.